Bali Travel Guide 2023

"Discovering the hidden gems of Bali: A comprehensive travel guide to its culture, cuisine, and essential tips to first time visitors on vacation"

James J. Johnson

Table of contents

Bali introduction

East of Java in Indonesia, on a small island province, is Bali. It is renowned for its breathtaking natural beauty, extensive cultural legacy, and thriving art scene. Travelers from all over the world flock to Bali to explore its pristine beaches, verdant rice terraces, and historic temples. Bali is a charming and unforgettable location because, despite its popularity, it has been able to preserve its distinctive personality and culture.

Location and Climate

Bali is situated in the Indonesian archipelago halfway between Java and Lombok. It has a total size of 5,780 square kilometers and is a member of the Lesser Sunda Islands. The island is made up of two main mountain ranges, the largest of which, Mount Agung, rises to a height of 3,031 meters. The island is volcanic in origin. Bali experiences two different seasons, rainy and dry, in a tropical environment. The dry season is from April to September, and the wet season is from October to March. The year-round average temperature, which ranges from 26 to 28 degrees Celsius, is generally stable.

Culture and History

Hindu influence has impacted Bali's unique and diverse culture for many years. Balinese culture is renowned for its ornate religious rituals, fine art, and traditional dance performances. In the 13th century, Bali was a member of the Majapahit Empire, which introduced Hinduism to the island. Thereafter, several petty kingdoms, including the potent Gelgel dynasty, which dominated the island during its heyday in the 16th century, came to power. Bali joined the Dutch East Indies in the 20th century and then Indonesia after that country's independence in 1945.

The rich arts culture of Bali, which features classical dance, music, and sculpture, is well-known today. Religion has had a significant influence on Balinese art, and many pieces feature scenes from the Mahabharata and Ramayana epics. Another significant aspect of the island's cultural legacy is Balinese dance. The most well-known of them is the Legong dance, which is done by little girls and is distinguished by its deft hand and eye gestures. The traditional gamelan music of Bali, which is performed on a variety of instruments such as xylophones, gongs, and drums, is also well-known.

Events and Festivals

Bali is well-known for its vibrant festivals and events, which are held all year long. These occasions offer a rare chance to encounter Balinese culture firsthand and are a favorite among many tourists who come to the island.

The most significant holiday in Bali is Nyepi Day, also referred to as the Day of Silence. It occurs in March on the day following the new moon and is observed by fasting, meditation, and total stillncss. Even the airport is shut down as the island goes into complete shutdown.

Galungan is a ten-day celebration honoring the triumph of good over evil. Every 210 days, penjor (bamboo poles) are hung outside of homes and temples to commemorate it. The event comes to a close on Kuningan, the day the spirits go to the heavens.

The night before Nyepi Day is known as Nyepi Eve and is a time for raucous celebrations. Large statues of devils are carried through the streets in what is known as the ogoh-ogoh parade. A night of dancing, music, and fireworks follows this.

Three-day festival honoring the best of Indonesian cuisine is called the Ubud Food Festival. There are cooking demonstrations, food tastings, and speeches by well-known chefs.

BaliSpirit Festival is a five-day event that honors dance, yoga, and music. The event comprises seminars and performances by both foreign and local artists, drawing visitors from all over the world.

On the beaches of the island, an event called the Kite Festival is held every year. Participants compete to fly the biggest and most inventive kite, and it features colorful kites of all sizes and shapes.

A traditional Balinese holiday called Tumpek Landep honors the metal god. Every six months, it is observed by blessing metal items like knives, automobiles, and computers.

Saraswati Day is a day set aside to celebrate the goddess of learning and knowledge. At temples and residences, flowers and books are offered as a symbol of the occasion.

Every June, a month-long festival called the Bali Arts Festival honors Balinese art and culture. It offers theatrical, musical, and dance acts as well as art exhibitions and regional cuisine.

The community of Tenganan hosts the unusual event known as Perang Pandan. Men with prickly pandan leaves engage in a fake battle in it. The celebration honors the village's 18th-century triumph over an advancing army.

Bali is a magical place with a distinctive fusion of stunning natural scenery, a deep cultural history, and a thriving arts scene. Bali has something to offer everyone, from its breathtaking beaches and rice terraces to its complex religious events and traditional dance performances. Festivals and other events held on the island give tourists a chance to get a close-up look at Balinese culture. Everyone who wants to experience Southeast Asia's beauty and diversity should travel to Bali.

Chapter 1: Arranging a Trip to Bali

Bali is a well-known travel destination in Indonesia, prized for its stunning beaches, paddy terraces, temples, and diverse culture. Before booking your travel, there are a few things to think about if you're planning a trip to Bali. The ideal time to visit Bali, transportation options, entry and visa requirements, and vacation planning are all covered in this book.

Bali Visit Season

The dry season, which lasts from May to September, is the ideal time to visit Bali. The ocean is quiet and clear, and the weather is dry and bright, making today the perfect time to go swimming, snorkeling, and surfing. This is a pleasant time to tour the island because the temperature is between 25 and 30 degrees Celsius.

Be ready for frequent downpours if you intend to travel to Bali during the rainy season, which lasts from October to April. Although the rain may come and go, it can occasionally last for days, which can result in flooding and mudslides. Yet, this is a popular time to visit Bali for tourists on a tight budget because it is less congested and hotel rates are lower.

Getting to Bali

Air travel is the most popular method of access to Bali. The primary entrance to the island of Bali is Ngurah Rai International Airport, which is situated in Denpasar, the island's capital. Major global hubs including Singapore, Kuala Lumpur, Bangkok, Sydney, and Melbourne all have direct flights to Bali.

You can also take a domestic flight to Bali from places like Jakarta, Surabaya, or Yogyakarta if you are already in Indonesia. As an alternative, you might take a ferry from one of the adjacent islands, such as Java or Lombok.

Entrance Requirements and Visas

For entry into Bali, you could require a visa, depending on your country of origin. For up to 30 days, citizens of a select group of nations—including those in the United States, Canada, Australia, and many parts of Europe—can enter Bali without a visa. But, you must apply for a visa in advance if your stay will be longer than 30 days.

You need a passport that will be valid for at least six months after your arrival date enters Bali. You might also be required to provide evidence of further travel, such as a return ticket or other documentation confirming travel to a different location.

The spending plan for Bali

Bali is a reasonably inexpensive travel destination with a variety of lodging alternatives, from inexpensive hostels to opulent villas. Yet how much your trip will cost depends depend on how you travel and what you want to accomplish. You can prepare your budget for your vacation to Bali using the anticipated expenditures below:

Accommodations: Mid-range hotels and guesthouses start at about $30–50 USD per night, but cheap hostels may be found for as little as $10–15 USD per night. A night's stay at a luxurious villa or resort might cost more than USD 200.

Food and drink prices range from $1 to USD 3 per meal at local eateries and cheap street food joints to $10 to USD 15 at mid-range eateries and cafés. High-end dining establishments and Western-style eateries often have dinner prices that exceed USD 50. A beer or drink bottle may cost between $3 and USD 8.

Transportation: Taxis and ride-hailing services are commonly available in Bali, and depending on the distance, a ride can cost anywhere from $5 to USD 20. Scooter rental costs typically range from $5 to USD 10 per day.

Activities: There is a broad range of prices for activities in Bali. In opposed to sports like surfing, snorkeling, and scuba diving, which can cost upwards of USD 50, entrance fees to temples and other sights can range from $1 to USD 5. Popular in Bali are spa services and massages, which can run you $15 to $30 per hour.

A budget tourist should budget $30 to USD 5 per day, whereas mid-range travelers should budget $50 to USD 100 per day. Luxurious travelers should budget more than USD 200 each day.

Activities in Bali

Visitors can choose from a variety of experiences and activities in Bali. Some of the top things to do in Bali are listed below:

See Temples - The island of Bali is renowned for its stunning Hindu temples, many of which are situated in picturesque settings near rice terraces, lakes, and the ocean. Uluwatu Temple, Tanah

Lot Temple, and Besakih Temple are a few of the most well-liked temples to visit.

Discover Ubud: Ubud is a town in the heart of Bali that is renowned for its arts and culture. You can explore the numerous local art galleries and museums, as well as the Ubud Palace and the Sacred Monkey Forest Sanctuary, here.

Unwind on the Beaches: Kuta Beach, Seminyak Beach, and Nusa Dua Beach are just a few of Bali's stunning coastline. Surfing, snorkeling, and scuba diving are among the water sports you may try out here along with relaxing in the sun and swimming in the ocean.

Visit Rice Terraces - Bali is renowned for its stunning rice terraces, which are also significant from a cultural perspective as they play a significant role in Balinese agriculture. Tegalalang Rice Terrace and Jatiluwih Rice Terrace are two of the most well-liked rice terraces to visit.

Go hiking - The island of Bali has many hiking paths that provide breathtaking views of the natural splendor of the place. Mountain hikes including Mount Batur, Mount Agung, and Campuhan Ridge Walk are among the most well-liked excursions.

Bali is a stunning and distinctive location that has plenty to offer to every kind of traveler. Bali has everything you might want from a relaxed beach trip to cultural activities to outdoor adventures. You can maximize your stay on this breathtaking island by properly organizing your trip and setting aside enough money.

Chapter 2: Top Bali Attractions

Bali is a magnificent island in Indonesia that is well-known for its vibrant culture, breathtaking scenery, and countless attractions. Bali has much to offer everyone, from historic temples and shrines to pristine beaches and extraordinary wildlife. Bali has everything you might want from an action-packed escape to a calm beach vacation. The major Bali attractions, including temples and shrines, beaches and water sports, animals and nature, art and culture, shopping and markets, and nightlife and entertainment, will be discussed in this article.

Shrines and Temples

For good reason, Bali is frequently referred to as the "Island of the Gods." Many historic temples and shrines may be found on the island, each of which has a distinct background and significance. The temples are a must-see sight for any Bali visitor because they are frequently accompanied by lovely gardens and breathtaking natural scenery.

The Tanah Lot Temple is one of Bali's most well-known temples. One of the most popular tourist destinations on the island is this temple, which is perched on a rocky outcrop in the middle of the ocean. Visitors can enjoy the breathtaking sunset views while watching the waves crash against the rocks at the temple, which is devoted to the Balinese sea gods.

The Uluwatu Temple is another well-known temple in Bali. This temple, which is perched on a cliff with a view of the ocean, doubles as a favorite place to watch the sunset. In the temple's amphitheater, visitors can also catch a traditional Balinese dancing performance in the evening.

The biggest and most significant temple in Bali is the Besakih Temple, sometimes referred to as the Mother Temple. The temple, which is perched atop Mount Agung, offers beautiful views of the surrounding area. The complex's several temples and shrines, including the Pura Penataran Agung, which honors the Hindu deity Shiva, are open to visitors to explore.

Watersports and Beaches

White sand shorelines and crystalline waters can be found on some of Bali's most stunning beaches. The island is a popular location for water sports like diving, snorkeling, and surfing.

Kuta Beach is one of Bali's most well-known beaches. This beach, which is in the center of Bali's tourism area, is renowned for its bustling vibe, great surf breaks, and breathtaking sunsets. Together with these sports, visitors can go parasailing, jet skiing, and banana boating.

Nusa Dua Beach is another well-liked beach in Bali. The waters at this beach are renowned for being crystal clear and excellent for swimming and snorkeling. The adjacent islands and reefs can also be explored by taking a boat cruise.

Sanur Beach is a fantastic choice for anyone seeking a more private beach experience. This beach, which lies on Bali's east coast, is less congested than other well-liked beaches on the island. Tourists can engage in a variety of water sports, such as kiteboarding and windsurfing.

Nature and wildlife

Bali is renowned for its magnificent animals and unspoiled landscapes. Bali is a naturalist's paradise, with everything from lush jungles to breathtaking waterfalls. A variety of animals, including monkeys, elephants, and rare bird species, can be seen at the island's numerous national parks and nature reserves, which are open to tourists.

The Bali Barat National Park is one of Bali's most well-known parks. Many animals inhabit this park, including deer, monkeys, and wild boar. The park's coral reefs, which are home to a diversity of marine life, including sea turtles and vibrant fish, can also be explored by visitors.

The Tegalalang Rice Terrace is another well-liked natural site in Bali. This terraced rice field, which can be seen in Bali's central highlands, is a magnificent illustration of traditional Balinese agriculture.

Tourists can explore the rice fields on foot or by bicycle while admiring the breathtaking views of the nearby mountains and jungle.

A trip to the Bali Safari and Marine Park is essential for everyone who wants to get up close and personal with Bali's distinctive fauna. More than 60 different types of animals live in this park, including tigers, elephants, and orangutans. The park's safari rides allow visitors to experience the animals in their natural settings.

Culture and the Arts

Bali's art and architecture are a reflection of its rich cultural heritage. The island's numerous museums and galleries, which include contemporary works by both local and foreign artists as well as traditional Balinese artwork, are open to visitors.

The Agung Rai Museum of Art is one of Bali's most well-known galleries. The goal of this museum is to preserve and advance Balinese art and culture. In addition to attending cultural events and workshops, visitors can browse the museum's collection of traditional paintings, sculptures, and textiles.

The Ubud Art Market is yet another well-liked art destination in Bali. The hub of Bali's cultural district of Ubud is home to this bustling market, which is a terrific spot to buy traditional Balinese artwork and handicrafts. The making of traditional batik textiles and other crafts can be observed by tourists.

A trip to the Pura Taman Saraswati Temple is essential for anybody interested in traditional Balinese architecture. This magnificent temple, which honors the goddess of learning, music, and the arts, is well known for its exquisite sculptures and lotus pond.

Markets and retail

With a variety of markets and shopping malls to suit all interests and budgets, Bali is a shopper's dream. Everyone can find something they want in Bali, from high-end couture to traditional handicrafts.

Seminyak Square is one of Bali's most well-liked shopping areas. Many multinational brands, as well as regional boutiques and artisan stores, may be found in this shopping center. A variety of dining alternatives are available for visitors, ranging from formal dining establishments to food trucks.

A trip to the Ubud Art Market is essential for anyone seeking a more convenient shopping experience. Batik textiles, wood carvings, silver jewelry, and other traditional Balinese handicrafts are all available at the kiosks in t a bustling market. To receive the greatest deals, customers can bargain with the suppliers.

Entertainment and Nightlife

With a wide selection of pubs, clubs, and eateries to suit all preferences, Bali boasts a thriving nighttime culture. Bali offers something for everyone, from beach clubs with live music to rooftop bars with breathtaking views.

The Potato Head Beach Club is one of Bali's most well-known nightclubs. This beach club, which is situated in Seminyak, is renowned for its gorgeous architecture, delectable cocktails, and live music events. A variety of entertainment opportunities are available for visitors, including DJ sets, live music, and cultural events.

The Sky Garden Bali is another well-liked nightlife location in Bali. This multi-level club has several bars and dance floors and is situated in the center of Kuta. From EDM to hip hop, visitors can listen to a variety of music and dance the night away.

Certainly, Bali is a place that has something to offer everyone, from magnificent beaches to historical temples and shrines, as well as wildlife, the natural world, art, and culture, as well as markets and shopping, as well as nightlife and entertainment. Bali is a must-visit location for any traveler because of its distinctive culture, stunning scenery, and countless attractions.

Chapter 3: 7-Day Bali Itinerary

Bali is a paradise island that has become well-known throughout the world because of its unmatched natural beauty, varied culture, and age-old customs. The island is in Indonesia and has beautiful scenery, incredible beaches, and a lot of vegetation. Travelers can discover the spirit of Bali by exploring the island's many districts over seven days.

Day 1: A tour of Ubud

The cultural center of Bali, Ubud, is home to a large number of art galleries, museums, and historic temples. Go to the Ubud Monkey Forest, a sanctuary for long-tailed macaques, first thing in the morning. With its tall trees and a chance to see these cheeky monkeys up close, the forest is a terrific area to enjoy a stroll.

The Tegalalang Rice Terrace, a famous location in Bali, should then be visited. Tegalalang's rice terraces are a sight to behold, and walking through them offers a singular experience. The terraces, which were constructed in the ninth century, are evidence of Bali's long agricultural history.

See the Ubud Palace in the afternoon, which served as the royal family of Bali's residence. The palace is a fantastic location to discover the history and traditional architecture of Bali. In addition, you can go to the Hindu shrine to the goddess of learning and the arts called the Saraswati Temple.

Seeing a Balinese dance performance is a must-do experience to round off your day. The dance performances, which feature Bali's traditional dance, music, and costumes, are held every night in Ubud.

Picturesque Journey to North Bali on Day 2

North Bali is an excellent place to get away from the crowds because it is less touristy than other areas of the island. Drive to the Gitgit Waterfall, a 40-meter waterfall surrounded by lush vegetation, to begin your day. It is one of Bali's most stunning waterfalls and an excellent place to cool off in the water.

The Munduk village, which boasts breathtaking vistas and a temperate climate, is the next stop. The town is an excellent area to go for a nature walk because it is surrounded by hills. In addition, you can go to the Munduk waterfall, a 25-meter cascade that makes a fantastic backdrop for pictures.

Drive to Lovina Beach, a black-sand beach on Bali's northern coast, in the afternoon. A nice area to unwind, swim, or observe dolphins is Lovina Beach. Many eateries and cafes that serve regional food can be found all along the coastline.

Day 3: Lovina's relaxation

Take a yoga session in the morning or indulge in a spa treatment to unwind on a quiet day in Lovina. It's easy to relax and get in touch with Bali's tranquil surroundings at Lovina. As an alternative, you might go to the Banjar Hot Springs, a natural hot spring surrounded by luscious vegetation. The hot springs are a fantastic location to unwind and revitalize your body.

Make your way to Bali's largest Buddhist temple, Brahma Vihara Arama, in the afternoon. The temple is renowned for its exquisite architecture and provides a calm setting for reflection or meditation. In addition, you may go to the 10-meter-tall Banjar Waterfall, which is an excellent place to swim.

Island hopping and snorkeling on Day 4

Visit Nusa Penida Island for the day; it is situated southeast of Bali. Nusa Penida is a fantastic location for island hopping and snorkeling because of its many stunning beaches and clean waters.

Take a boat to the Angel's Billabong, an oceanfront natural infinity pool, to start your day. The Bill Abong is a well-liked location for photographs and a fantastic site for a swim.

Next, proceed to Broken Beach, a natural cove encircled by tall rocks. Broken Beach is a wonderful location for a stroll while taking in the breathtaking ocean views.

Take a boat to Crystal Bay in the afternoon, which is renowned for its crystal-clear waters and a variety of marine life. Manta rays and reef sharks are among the many fish species you might view at Crystal Bay when snorkeling. You can also go to Kelingking Beach, which is distinguished by a special rock formation in the shape of a T-Rex.

On Day 5, go to East Bali.

East Bali is an excellent site to learn about Bali's history and customs because it is where Bali's historical and cultural heritage can be found. The Besakih Temple, Bali's biggest and most significant Hindu temple, is a good place to start your day. The temple, which is situated on Mount Agung's slopes, is an excellent spot to learn about Bali's spiritual customs.

The Tirta Gangga Water Palace is the next stop; it is a lovely water garden surrounded by tropical vegetation and fish ponds. It's wonderful to stroll around the palace and soak in the serene atmosphere.

Visit the Taman Ujung Water Palace in the afternoon, which is another lovely water park encircled by a sizable pond. The palace is a wonderful area to promenade and take in the breathtaking seaside views.

Day 6: Jimbaran Sunset Dinner

Jimbaran is a wonderful location for a romantic beachside dinner and is well-known for its breathtaking views of the setting sun. Visit the Hindu shrine, Uluwatu Temple, which is perched on a cliff overlooking the ocean, first thing in the morning. The temple is a wonderful location to learn about Bali's religious customs and take in the breathtaking ocean views.

Next, proceed to Dreamland Beach, a well-known surfing location with white sand beaches and crystal-clear waters. A nice spot to unwind and swim is the beach.

In the evening, visit Jimbaran Bay, which is renowned for its eateries serving up local seafood. Jimbaran Bay is a wonderful location for a romantic beachside dinner and sunset viewing.

Day 7: Seminyak Beach Day

Seminyak is a fantastic destination to end your Bali vacation because of its exciting nightlife and gorgeous beaches. Visit the Hindu temple Tanah Lot, which is situated on a rocky outcrop in the sea, first thing in the morning. The temple is a wonderful location to take in the breathtaking ocean views and discovers Bali's religious customs.

Next, proceed to Seminyak Beach, a well-liked location for surfing and tanning. Several beach clubs and eateries that serve regional food can be found along the beach. As an alternative, you might go to the Potato Head Beach Club, a well-known beach club with breathtaking ocean views.

The Ku De Ta Beach Club, which is renowned for its exciting nightlife and live music performances, is a great place to go in the evening. The beach club is a fantastic location to sip on a cocktail while admiring the mesmerizing sunset views.

Bali is a paradise island that provides visitors with a wide range of activities and attractions. A seven-day plan allows visitors to explore Bali's natural beauty, culture, and history by traveling to various parts of the island.

Chapter 4: Bali's transportation alternatives

Indonesia is home to the well-known tourist resort of Bali. It is renowned for its breathtaking landscapes, vibrant culture, and gorgeous beaches. Visitors to Bali have a variety of alternatives for getting around, including taxis, ride-sharing services, public transportation, car and motorbike rentals, and more. Each of these choices will be thoroughly covered in this essay, along with its advantages and disadvantages.

Using a car and a motorcycle to get around Bali

Renting a car or motorcycle is one of the most common ways to navigate Bali. Visitors have the choice and freedom to explore the island at their speed with both alternatives. Yet, it is crucial to keep in mind that driving in Bali can be difficult, particularly for people who are not accustomed to operating a vehicle on the left side of the road.

Also, traffic can be congested, particularly in populated regions like Kuta and Denpasar.

There are various choices available for tourists renting a car or motorcycle in Bali. In addition to the numerous rental agencies spread out around the island, several hotels and resorts also provide rental services. Depending on the kind of vehicle, the length of the rental, and the rental agency, the cost to rent a car or motorcycle varies. Visitors should budget between $20 and $30 per day to rent a motorcycle and between $30 and $50 per day to rent a car.

Utilizing Bali's public transportation

Bali's public transportation system isn't as developed as it is elsewhere in the world. For those who do not want to rent a car or a motorcycle, there are several alternatives.

Bemos: In Bali, tiny minivans known as bemos are the main mode of public transportation. They run on set itineraries and are frequently crammed. Depending on the distance, bemo rides can be expensive, but they are typically quite cheap, with rates starting at about $0.50.

Buses: Many bus routes travel the entire island of Bali. These buses provide a more comfortable ride than Bemos and are typically air-conditioned. They cost more and are less common, with rates beginning at about $1.

Bali's taxis and ride-sharing services

Bali has both taxis and ride-sharing services. Visitors should be advised, nevertheless, that not all cabs have meters, and some may try to overcharge foreigners. However, although they are still extensively utilized, ride-sharing services like Uber and Grab are officially forbidden in Bali.

Metered Taxis: In Bali, there are several metered taxi services, such as Blue Bird, Bali Taksi, and Kura-Kura. The fares are metered, and these cabs are typically trustworthy and safe. Visitors should be warned that it can be challenging to get a metered taxi during rush hour and that some drivers may choose not to utilize the meter.

Non-Metered Taxis: Non-metered taxis are also offered in Bali, albeit they are frequently more expensive. To avoid being overcharged, customers should haggle the fare before boarding the taxi.

Although they are legally illegal, ride-sharing services like Uber and Grab are frequently used in Bali. Tourists should be warned that some drivers could be reluctant to take up visitors due to the possibility of fines or other consequences.

Transportation costs in Bali

Depending on the mode of transportation and the distance traveled transportation costs change in Bali. The average prices for each choice are broken out as follows:

Hire a motorcycle for $20–$30 per day.
$30 to $50 per day for a rental car

Bemo: $0.50 to $1 for each ride
$1–$2 for each bus travel
Taxi with a meter: $0.50 to $1 per kilometer

Taxi Without Meter

Whether going long distances or frequently using taxis, the expense of transportation in Bali can add up rapidly. In Bali, there are ways to reduce your transportation expenses. Visitors can, for instance, rent a car or motorcycle for a longer period, which could result in a lower daily charge. To avoid being overcharged, travelers might haggle with taxi drivers about the rate.

Advice for navigating Bali

Here are some suggestions for getting about if you're thinking about visiting Bali:

If you are accustomed to driving on the left side of the road and are familiar with Bali's traffic, rent a motorbike or a car.

Where possible, take a metered taxi; otherwise, haggle the fee before boarding a non-metered vehicle.

Though theoretically banned in Bali, ride-sharing services like Uber and Grab might be used.

If you plan to take public transit, be ready for crowded demos and sporadic bus service.

If you are renting a motorcycle, always wear a helmet and check sure the brakes and lights are operational.

Get to know the horn usage and hand signals as well as the local traffic regulations and customs.

Bali can be difficult to navigate, but with the appropriate knowledge and preparation, tourists can travel the island economically and safely. Consider the expenses and advantages of each choice before deciding whether to take a taxi, take public transportation, or rent a car or motorcycle. You can make the most of your trip to Bali and explore everything this lovely island has to offer by keeping in mind these suggestions and being organized.

Chapter 5: Accommodations in Bali

Bali is a well-liked vacation spot in Indonesia recognized for its exquisite beaches, breathtaking scenery, and distinctive culture. From cheap backpackers to luxury seekers, it offers a variety of lodging options to suit their needs. In this post, we'll look at the different types of lodging options in Bali, as well as the most well-liked neighborhoods for lodging.

Accommodations Available in Bali

Bali provides a wide variety of lodging options to accommodate different types of visitors. Some of Bali's most popular lodging options are listed below:

Hotels: Bali offers a wide range of lodging options, from inexpensive to opulent. The majority of hotels have amenities including restaurants, spas, and swimming pools.

Villas: Bali is renowned for its opulent villas, which provide seclusion, comfort, and a distinctive experience. Most villas have gardens, pools, and personnel to take care of your requirements.

Guesthouses: Guesthouses are inexpensive lodging options with standard amenities like a bed, a fan, and a bathroom. These are a fantastic choice for vacationers on a tight budget who don't require upscale amenities.

Hostels - Budget and backpacker visitors frequently stay in hostels. They provide dormitory-style lodging with communal amenities and bathrooms.

Homestays: Homestays are a wonderful way to get to know the locals and experience their culture. They include meals and provide simple lodging at a family's home.

Resorts - Bali is home to a large number of opulent resorts with top-notch amenities like spas, restaurants, and private beaches. They are a fantastic option for anyone who wants to relax and live a life of luxury.

Bungalows – These independent homes provide a more genuine Balinese experience. They often offer limited facilities and are constructed from natural materials like wood and thatch.

Bali's Most Popular Places to Stay

Bali features several well-liked lodging options, each providing a distinctive experience. Some of the most well-liked places to stay in Bali are listed below:

Kuta is a popular neighborhood in Bali known for its shopping, surfing, and nightlife. It is well-liked by youthful tourists and provides a selection of lodging options for every price range.

Seminyak is a popular neighborhood in Bali noted for its posh restaurants, beach clubs, and opulent homes. Families and couples seeking a more upmarket experience frequently use it.

The cultural center of Bali, Ubud, is well-known for its temples, rice paddies, and open-air marketplaces. It is well-liked by tourists who wish to fully experience Balinese culture and spirituality.

Nusa Dua is a posh neighborhood in Bali noted for its opulent resorts, championship golf courses, and exclusive beaches. It is well-liked by couples on their honeymoons and those looking to splurge on luxury.

Canggu is a relaxed neighborhood in Bali that is well-known for its vegan eateries, yoga studios, and surfing. It is well-liked by surfers, digital nomads, and others seeking a more laid-back atmosphere.

Accommodations in Bali on a Budget

Bali offers a variety of affordable lodging options, making it a fantastic destination for those on a tight budget. Here are some of Bali's top low-cost lodgings:

Hotels in capsules - For tourists on a tight budget who value comfort and privacy, hotels in capsules are a fantastic choice. They provide lodging in the form of capsules with communal facilities and bathrooms.

Guesthouses - For tourists on a tight budget looking for simple lodging, guesthouses are a perfect choice. These are typically found in the middle of the city and come with a bed, fan, and bathroom.

Hostels - Backpackers and tourists on a tight budget frequently choose hostels. They provide dormitory-style lodging with communal amenities and bathrooms.

Hostels - Hostels

Affordable accommodations - Numerous hotels in Bali are affordable and include standard features like a bed, a fan or air conditioner, and a toilet. These are excellent choices for people who want comfort and solitude without spending a fortune.

Bungalows - For travelers on a budget who want a more genuine Balinese experience, bungalows are a terrific choice. They often offer limited facilities and are constructed from natural materials like wood and thatch.

Camping is a fantastic choice for intrepid visitors who want to discover Bali's natural beauty. In Bali, many campgrounds provide tents and simple amenities.

Bali's High-End Accommodations

Bali is renowned for its opulent lodgings that provide top-notch amenities and services. Some of Bali's top luxury hotels are listed below:

Private Villas: Bali is home to a large number of opulent private villas that provide seclusion, comfort, and breathtaking views. They have workers who can attend to your requirements, private pools, and gardens.

Resorts - Bali is home to several top-notch resorts with amenities like restaurants, spas, and private beaches. They are a fantastic option for anyone who wants to relax and live a life of luxury.

Boutique hotels: Bali is home to a large number of opulent boutique hotels that provide customized services and one-of-a-kind experiences. They are a fantastic choice for anyone seeking an alternative to typical chain hotels.

Beachfront homes - Bali is home to a large number of opulent beachfront homes that provide spectacular ocean views and easy access to the beach. They are a fantastic choice for people who want to vacation at the beach in luxury.

Wellness retreats: Many wellness retreats in Bali provide yoga, meditation, and spa services. They are a fantastic choice for people who wish to refresh their bodies, mind, and spirit.

From cheap backpackers to luxury seekers, Bali offers a variety of lodging options to suit their needs. Bali has accommodations for all budgets, whether you want a lavish villa or a modest guesthouse. Budget, preferred location, and the kind of experience you're looking for should all be taken into account when selecting a place to stay in Bali. With so many choices, it will be easy for you to select the ideal lodging for your Bali vacation.

Chapter 6: Bali's Dinner Scene

Bali, an island in Indonesia, is well known for its stunning scenery, exciting culture, and mouthwatering cuisine. Traditional Balinese cuisine, worldwide favorites, street food, and fine dining establishments are all available on the island, reflecting the diversity of its population. We'll look at the several dining options Bali has to offer in this article.

Traditional cuisine of Bali

Indian, Chinese, and Indonesian elements are combined to create Balinese food. Often, the meal is hot and has a salty, sweet, and sour flavor profile. The most popular dishes consist of:

A meal of rice accompanied by a variety of side dishes, including chicken, meat, veggies, and sambal (spicy sauce).

Babi Guling is a stuffed, spit-roasted suckling pig that is eaten with rice and veggies.

Bebek Betutu is a spice-stuffed duck that is baked in banana leaves.
Lawar is a rice-paired salad salad-comporatcompoonut, veggies, and ground beef.

Sate is grilled beef, hog, or chicken on skewers with peanut sauce.
Chicken soup with noodles, veggies, and spices is known as soto ayam.
Across the entire island, these meals can be found in regional eateries and warungs (small food stands).

Favorite Cuisines Throughout the World

As varied as Bali's traditional food is its international food scene. There are a lot of restaurants on the island that provide different types of international food, like Italian, Japanese,

Chinese, and Mediterranean. The following are some of the most well-liked international dishes:

Thin-crust pizza with a variety of toppings, including Margherita, pepperoni, and Hawaiian.
Sushi is rice and raw fish served in bite-sized quantities with wasabi and soy sauce.
Served with lime wedges, pad Thai is a stir-fried noodle meal with veggies, pork, and peanuts.

Burgers are a type of sandwich that typically come with fries and a beef or vegetarian patty, as well as lettuce, tomato, and cheese.
Kebabs are eaten with pita bread and feature grilled skewered meat, veggies, and sauces.

Tacos: Soft or hard tacos with a variety of meats, veggies, and sauces.
These dishes may be found in a variety of eateries and cafés across the island, especially in popular tourist destinations like Kuta and Seminyak.

Local markets and fast-food joints

Try the street food and local markets in Bali for a more genuine and affordable dining experience. A broad range of meals are available at reasonable costs at street food stands and neighborhood markets, including:

Rice and veggies are served with a suckling pig that has been grilled on a spit.
Nasi Goreng: Crackers are served with fried rice that includes veggies, meat, and an egg.
Fried noodles with veggies, pork, and eggs served with crackers are known as Mie Goreng.

Bakso is a vegetable and meatball soup with noodles.
A salad comprised of tofu, cooked veggies, and peanut sauce is known as gado-gado.

Fried banana fritters with chocolate sauce are known as pisang goreng.
On the island, you may find these meals in a variety of street food stands and local markets, especially in Denpasar and Ubud.

Upscale dining and culinary adventures

Bali has many fine dining establishments and culinary experiences for those seeking a more opulent dining experience. These eateries frequently have chefs with Michelin stars and offer a combination of regional and global flavors. The following are a few of Bali's most well-liked fine dining establishments and culinary experiences:

A restaurant featuring a blend of traditional and contemporary Balinese food is called a locavore since it emphasizes the use of seasonal and local ingredients in its meals.

2. Mozaic - This eatery serves a special tasting menu that combines French cuisine with spices from Bali.

A beautiful and opulent restaurant serving Mediterranean fare is called Kubu, and it is situated by the Ayung River.

A beachside restaurant and lounge called KU DE TA serve a variety of international and Asian dishes in addition to beverages and live music.

A plant-based restaurant serving vegan and vegetarian fare, Sakti Dining Room focuses on using organic, locally sourced ingredients.

Cooking courses are provided by a lot of Bali's hotels and eateries, allowing tourists to learn how to prepare native cuisine while also shopping at nearby markets.

From international favorites, street food, and fine dining options to traditional Balinese cuisine, Bali's dining scene has something to offer everyone. Indulge in one of the many fine dining establishments and culinary experiences the island has to offer or explore the local markets and street food vendors for an authentic and affordable dining experience. Whatever your tastes, Bali's food culture is certain to satisfy you and leave you wanting more.

Chapter 7: Bali Shopping

The breathtaking beaches, magnificent temples, and vibrant culture of Bali are well recognized. Yet the island is also a shopping haven, with everything from customary arts and crafts to upscale clothing and luxury items. Bali has something for everyone, whether you're seeking for gifts to take home or indulging in some real retail therapy.

Crafts and arts from the past

Bali is renowned for its indigenous arts and crafts, which are strongly ingrained in the Hindu culture of the island. The most well-liked products include:

Wax and dye are used in the traditional process of batik to print on fabric. Clothing, tablecloths, and other decorative objects are frequently made from batik.

Woodcarvings: The elaborate woodcarvings produced in Bali are well-known and frequently used to adorn temples and other places of worship. Anything from little carvings to enormous, elaborate sculptures can be found.

Silver jewelry: Bali is known for its complex, handcrafted jewelry and is home to some of the best silversmiths in the world.

Traditional textiles: Bali has a long history of weaving, and you can discover a wide range of vibrant textiles there, including endek, songket, and ikat.

Masks and puppets are used in Balinese traditional dance performances and make excellent mementos. They frequently have vivid colors and are very detailed.

There are many markets and shops in Bali that specialize in traditional arts and crafts if you're interested in buying any. Among the most well-liked shopping destinations are:

Ubud Market: The traditional arts and crafts seen in this lively market in the center of Ubud are world-famous. Everything is available, including wood sculptures, Balinese masks, and batik apparel.

One of the biggest markets in Bali is the Sukawati Art Market, which is situated not far from Ubud. It's an excellent location to buy jewelry, textiles, and other traditional goods.

The Kuta Art Market is a fantastic spot to buy souvenirs and is situated right in the center of Kuta. Everything is available, including t-shirts, wooden carvings, and Balinese masks.

Gifts and mementos

There are many choices if you're seeking presents and souvenirs to take home from Bali. Popular products include:

Balinese Coffee: Bali is well-known for its coffee, and the entire island's markets and shops sell a range of locally grown beans.

Bali Salt is a wonderful present for foodies and is gathered from the island's crystal-clear waters.

Handicrafts: Authentic handicrafts like woodcarvings, masks, and batik clothes are wonderful gifts.

Spa Products: Bali is well-known for its spas, and there are many locally created spa items available, like body washes and massage oils.

Items Made From Coconuts: Coconuts are widely available in Bali, and many items made from coconuts are also available, including coconut oil and coconut shell bowls.

There are several marketplaces and businesses in Bali that specialize in souvenirs and presents if you're shopping for these things. Among the most well-liked shopping destinations are:

Ubud Market: Ubud Market is an excellent area to purchase gifts and souvenirs in addition to traditional arts and crafts.

Seminyak Village is a posh shopping district in Seminyak that houses a selection of luxury stores and boutiques as well as some fantastic gift shops.

Beachside Markets: Kuta Beach and Sanur Beach are just two of Bali's many beaches that offer marketplaces where you may buy presents and souvenirs. These markets are fantastic places to find beachwear, sarongs, and other beach-related things.

Bali's High-End Shopping

Bali offers a wide range of possibilities if you're looking for upscale goods and clothing. Some of the most well-liked locations to buy high-end goods are:

Some of the island's top stores and boutiques may be found in Seminyak, a posh area of Bali. There are several top-tier fashion labels to choose from, as well as some fantastic stores for home furnishings.

Kuta: Kuta is well-known for its shopping, and the city's malls and shopping centers are home to a wide selection of upscale stores and boutiques.

Some of Bali's most opulent resorts are located in Nusa Dua, which is also home to several upmarket stores and boutiques that cater to affluent tourists.

It's vital to keep in mind that pricing in Bali can be more expensive than in other regions of Southeast Asia if you're seeking premium items. But, you may frequently save money on expensive products by haggling and negotiating a little.

Price haggling and bargaining

Prices are frequently negotiated and bartered in Bali, particularly in markets and smaller stores. The following advice will help you find the greatest offers:

Start with a modest offer: It's critical to begin bargaining with a low offer. This allows you to haggle and may result in a lower price.

Be courteous: Bargaining in Bali may be a nice and enjoyable experience, but it's crucial to be kind and respectful at all times.

Know the item's value before you begin to haggle: It's critical to know the item's value before you begin to haggle. This may aid in negotiating a reasonable price.

If necessary, go away if you're not satisfied with the asking price. The merchant will frequently call you back and present a lower price.

Negotiating is usual in Bali, and sellers expect it. Don't be scared to do it. Negotiating is frequently the greatest method to get a decent deal, so don't be scared to do it.

Overall, shopping in Bali can be enjoyable and rewarding, whether you're seeking high-end luxury goods, souvenirs and gifts, or traditional arts and crafts. You may frequently find fantastic prices on the products you're looking for with a little haggling and negotiating, adding to the fun of your shopping trip.

Chapter 8: Bali Health & Safety

One of the most well-liked travel locations in the world is Bali, sometimes referred to as the Isle of the Gods. It is not surprising that Bali draws millions of tourists each year given its beautiful beaches, vibrant culture, and welcoming locals. To guarantee a safe and pleasurable journey, travelers need to take a few health and safety precautions, just like they would in any other popular tourist location. This post will go over some general frauds and tourist traps to stay away from, as well as the health and safety precautions visitors to Bali should take.

Vaccinations and health precautions:

It is critical to follow some basic health precautions before visiting Bali. These safety measures include maintaining excellent hygiene, receiving the required immunizations, and taking malaria prophylaxis if necessary.

For visitors to Bali, the following immunizations are advised:

All visitors to Bali are advised to get the hepatitis A vaccine since it is spread by tainted food and water.

Typhoid: Due to the disease's transmission through tainted food and water, this vaccination is also advised for all visitors to Bali.

All travelers are advised to get tetanus and diphtheria vaccinations since these diseases are spread through polluted water and soil.

For travelers who were born after 1956, have never had the disease, or have not received the MMR vaccine, these shots are advised.

Hepatitis B vaccination is advised for tourists who could engage in sexual activity with locals, receive medical care, or engage in any other activities that could expose them to blood or bodily fluids.

Travelers who may be exposed to animals, such as dogs and monkeys, are advised to get the rabies vaccine.

Travelers should take malaria prophylaxis if necessary in addition to receiving the recommended vaccinations. Bali has malaria in several regions, particularly in the countryside. To establish whether they require malaria prophylaxis, travelers should speak with their healthcare physician.

Finally, visitors to Bali should maintain decent hygiene. This includes constantly washing your hands, consuming bottled water, and staying away from raw or undercooked foods.

Safety Advice for Bali Travel:

Although Bali is generally a secure destination for tourists, there are several security measures that visitors should take to guarantee a safe journey.

Drive with caution: Bali's roads can be hazardous, especially for inexperienced drivers. Instead, it is preferable to hire a driver or use a cab.

Pickpocketing occurs frequently in busy places like markets and tourist destinations. Secure your belongings, and pay attention to your surroundings.

Scams abound in Bali, including those involving bogus tour guides, exorbitantly priced trinkets, and counterfeit money. Always use caution while interacting with strangers, and bargain for a better deal before purchasing anything.

Keep an eye on your belongings at all times because theft is an issue in Bali. Never leave your valuables unattended and always keep them close to you.

Swim with caution; Bali's currents can be strong, especially during the wet season. Be mindful of the weather conditions and only swim in locations that are designated.

Bali is a highly religious and cultural place, therefore respect them. When visiting temples or other religious locations, dress modestly and pay respect to regional norms.

Typical tourist traps and scams

Although Bali is a stunning location, it is also notorious for its tourist traps and con artists. To avoid, be aware of the following scams and tourist traps:

False tour guides: There are a lot of persons in Bali who will offer to be your guide, but they could not be authorized or informed about the area. Always pick a reputable tour operator or a qualified tour guide.

Be cautious while buying souvenirs, especially in markets and popular tourist locations. Always haggle over the price and know what the thing is worth.

Taxis with malfunctioning meters: Certain taxis in Bali may be equipped with malfunctioning meters or chauffeurs who choose not to utilize them, resulting in an inflated rate. Always hire a trustworthy taxi service, and demand that the driver runs the meter.

Scams involving currency exchange: Be cautious when exchanging currencies as certain locations may advertise a reduced exchange rate or phony money. Use a trustworthy exchange facility at all times, and verify the exchange rate.

Timeshare presentations: A complimentary tour or supper may be provided by some hotels and resorts in Bali in exchange for attending a timeshare presentation. These presentations, however, might be aggressive sales pitches. If you aren't sincerely interested in buying a timeshare, stay away from their presentations.

Monkey Woods: Bali is renowned for having monkey forests, although these locations can be hazardous. If you agitate the monkeys or have food nearby, they can attack you. Be cautious and adhere to the staff's instructions.

Indeed, Bali is a stunning location that draws millions of visitors every year. To ensure a safe and pleasurable journey, it is necessary to take a few health and safety precautions. Tourists should practice good hygiene, acquire the required immunizations, and take malaria prophylaxis if necessary. Travelers should avoid driving, stay cautious of pickpockets and con artists, and observe local customs to ensure their safety.

Last but not least, travelers should be mindful of frequent frauds and tourist traps including impostor tour guides, exorbitant souvenir prices, and fraudulent currency exchanges. Travelers can have a secure and pleasurable journey to Bali by paying attention to these suggestions.

Chapter 9: Bali Traditional Etiquette

Between Java and Lombok sits the Indonesian province of Bali. The island is a well-liked vacation spot, renowned for its stunning beaches, scenic surroundings, and cultural activities. To respect local culture and prevent insulting locals, visitors to Bali should be knowledgeable of the customs and traditions of the area.

Modesty and the Dress Code

Bali's dress code and modesty rules are among the most crucial things to be aware of. Bali is an island with a large Hindu population, and the people there take their religious traditions and beliefs very seriously. When visiting temples and other religious sites, visitors to Bali are required to dress modestly and with respect.

Both men and women are supposed to cover their shoulders and legs when entering temples. This entails donning long, knee-length slacks or skirts and shoulder-covering tops. Visitors may also need to wear a sarong or sash, which are available at the temple.

It's crucial to dress modestly when exploring different areas of Bali. Avoid wearing clothes that are overly provocative or revealing, including shorts, tank tops, or low-cut shirts. Women should also avoid wearing bikinis or swimsuits in public locations, such as on the street or in shops.

Observing religious customs

As previously said, Bali is a largely Hindu island, and the inhabitants are highly serious about their religious activities. Respect for local traditions and practices is expected of visitors to Bali, especially when it comes to religion.

It's crucial to respect and be cognizant of regional traditions and customs when visiting temples. This includes taking off your shoes before entering the temple, dressing appropriately, and refraining from photographing people or holy items without their consent.

In terms of daily living, tourists should be informed of the regional traditions and customs. For instance, daily offerings of flowers, rice, and other goods to the gods are typical among the inhabitants. Visitors should treat these offerings with respect and refrain from trampling on them or otherwise upsetting them.

Local traditions and customs

Bali has a strong cultural legacy, and the island is home to numerous distinctive traditions and rituals. To respect the local way of life and prevent insulting the natives, visitors visiting Bali should be aware of certain traditions and customs.

The "Tri Hita Karana" custom, which translates as "the three causes of happiness," is one of Bali's most significant traditions. The belief that happiness is attained through the harmony and balance of three elements—namely, the relationships between people and their fellow humans, with the gods, and with nature—is referred to here.

This idea should be understood by visitors to Bali, and they should make an effort to respect the traditions and practices of the locals. This entails preserving the ecosystem and refraining from actions that could degrade the island's scenic appeal.

The celebration of "Nyepi," the Balinese New Year, is another significant custom in Bali. The entire island closes down for Nyepi, and everyone is obligated to spend the entire day inside. Visitors should be mindful of this custom and make travel arrangements appropriately.

Together with these customs, Bali is renowned for its distinctive arts and crafts. To find handcrafted items like batik garments, wood carvings, and silver jewelry, tourists to Bali should take the time to browse the neighborhood markets and shops.

Bali is a stunning, culturally diverse location that provides travelers with a distinctive experience. To respect the culture and prevent insulting the residents, tourists must be knowledgeable of the regional customs and traditions. Visitors can have a safe and happy journey to Bali by dressing modestly, respecting religious beliefs, and being aware of local customs and traditions.

Chapter 10: Language hints for Bali.

Communication and Language in Bali

Bali, a stunning island in Indonesia, is a well-liked travel destination for visitors from all over the world. Balinese is the native tongue of the Balinese people, however Indonesian is the official language used in Bali. Speaking both Indonesian and Balinese, the majority of Balinese people are multilingual. Basic Balinese phrases, communication strategies, and the use of technology and translation tools will all be covered in this essay.

Balinese language basics:

It's often beneficial to learn a few basic Balinese words before traveling to Bali so that you can connect with the natives. You might find the following Balinese expressions to be helpful:

Greetings, Om Swastiastu (om was-tee-as)
Greetings, Rahajeng Semeng (ra-ha-jeng se-meng)
Thank you, Suksma, and good day, Rahajeng Wengi (ra-ha-jeng wen-gi) (suk-sma)
Sure, Iya (ee-ya)
Not at all (ti-dak)
I'm sorry, Maaf (ma-af)
The amount? - What is the rate? Where is... (be-ra-pa har-ga-nya)? – Di mana? Do you know how to speak English? - Are you capable of speaking English? English: a-pa-kah an-da bi-sa be-ra-ca-ra ba-ha-sa
Communication Advice About Linguistic Barriers:

Language obstacles might persist even if the majority of Balinese are bilingual in Indonesian and Balinese. The following advice can help you efficiently interact with the locals:

Acquire a few basic words and phrases - As was already mentioned, being able to converse with the natives is made much easier by knowing a few fundamental Balinese words and phrases.

Even if the locals can understand you, speaking too quickly or with a strong accent can make it harder for them to understand. Speak slowly and clearly.

Employ gestures and facial expressions to help you communicate - If you're having difficulties getting your point across, consider using gestures and facial expressions.

Be patient – Keep in mind that language barriers might make communication difficult and time-consuming. Be patient and resist getting impatient if it takes a little longer to communicate your point.
using translation apps and technology:

Technology may be a fantastic tool for overcoming language barriers in the modern digital era. Here are some ways that technology can improve your ability to communicate in Bali:

Apps for translation - You may convert Balinese sentences into English or vice versa using a variety of translation applications. Google Translate and iTranslate are two common choices.

Apps for language learning: If you're planning a longer stay in Bali, you might want to use a program like Duolingo to learn Balinese.

Social media - For connecting with locals and learning about events and activities in Bali, social media sites like Facebook and Instagram might be helpful.

Internet forums - Online forums like TripAdvisor can be an excellent tool for connecting with other travelers who have been to Bali and gaining travel tips.

Due to the language barrier, communicating properly in Bali can be difficult, but it is most definitely feasible with a little effort. Language obstacles can be addressed by learning a few simple Balinese words and phrases, communicating slowly, using gestures and facial expressions, and being patient.

Technology may also be a tremendous tool for communication, whether it be through the use of social media platforms, online forums, language learning apps, or translation software. You may make your trip to Bali considerably more pleasurable and successful by using these tactics.

Although Indonesian and Balinese are the two main languages used in Bali, English is also frequently spoken there, especially in tourist regions. To interact with tourists, many residents in Bali who work in the tourism sector have acquired English language skills. Yet, when traveling, it's usually kind and welcome to try to speak the local tongue.

It's critical to be aware of how cultural differences can affect communication in Bali in addition to linguistic limitations. Being respectful and avoiding conflict is vital since Balinese culture values peace and respect. It's vital to pay attention to nonverbal clues and tone of voice when communicating with Balinese people because they may be more oblique in their communication.

Ultimately, for a successful trip to Bali, efficient communication is crucial. Language obstacles can be surmounted and you can engage with Bali's native culture by learning a few simple phrases, using technology, and being aware of cultural variances.

Chapter 11: Bali Money and Tipping

Currency & Exchange Rates for Money and Tipping in Bali

The Indonesian Rupiah is the currency used in Bali, which is a part of Indonesia (IDR). The IDR is offered in coins ranging from 50 to 1,000 and banknotes ranging from 1,000 to 100,000. Although the exchange rate is volatile, as of April 2023, 1 USD is roughly equivalent to 14,000 IDR. It is usually advised to research the most recent exchange rates before departing for Bali.

Banks, money exchangers, and hotels are just a few locations in Bali where you can convert money. The best place to exchange money is at a trustworthy bank or money changer, though. Bali has numerous money changers that are easily identified by their signage that display the current currency rates. Even though some money changers may offer a better rate than others, it is crucial to avoid falling victim to fraud. Before leaving the money changer, always count your money and verify the exchange rate.

Bali has ATMs and credit cards.

In Bali, credit cards are generally accepted, particularly in bigger facilities like hotels, restaurants, and retail stores. It is usually advised to have cash on hand, though, as many marketplaces and smaller shops might only accept cash. It is crucial to keep in mind that some companies might impose a fee for credit card use, so it is always advisable to verify with the company first.

Also, there are ATMs spread all across Bali, making it simple to withdraw money in the native currency. Banks, supermarkets, and shopping malls all have ATMs. It is crucial to be aware that some ATMs may charge a fee for withdrawals, and that using ATMs within banks or retail malls is always advised for safety reasons.

Customs and Rules for Tipping

Although not required in Bali, tips are often appreciated. It's vital to keep in mind that Bali has lower living expenses than most Western nations, thus any tip offered will likely make a big difference to the recipient. Tipping is especially valued in the service sector, which includes establishments like hotels, spas, and restaurants.

Some tips for tipping in Bali:

Restaurants: A service fee of 10% is typically included in the bill for Bali's eateries. This signifies that tipping is welcomed but not required. You might choose to tip an extra 5–10% if you experience great service.

Hotels: Although tipping is not required, it is appreciated. It is usual to give the housekeeping workers and the bellhop who brings your bags to your room a little gratuity. For the housekeeping crew, a modest tip of about 10,000 IDR per day is adequate, and for the bellhop, a tip of between 20,000 and 50,000 IDR is suitable.

Spas: Tipping is not required but is always appreciated at spas. It is usual to give the masseuse who performs the treatment a little gratuity. 10% or so as a modest gratuity is appropriate.

Drivers and tour guides: Tipping drivers and tour guides are not required, but it is appreciated. Depending on the quality of the service, a little gratuity of between 50,000 and 100,000 IDR every day as usual.

Additional services: Tipping is not required, however, it is appreciated, for example, for hair stylists, manicurists, and taxi drivers. 10% or so as a modest gratuity is appropriate.

It is crucial to remember that the aforementioned recommendations are just that—recommendations. Tipping is an individual choice, and the amount should always be based on the caliber of the service received. It's also crucial to keep your spending in check and leave tips that you can afford. It is preferable to leave a tiny gratuity rather than none at all.

It's also crucial to keep in mind that, despite being appreciated, tipping is not customary in Bali. In general, Bali's residents are warm and welcoming, and they cheerfully render services whether or not they are tipped.

Bali is a fantastic holiday destination, but it's crucial to respect the local conventions about payment and tipping. Always carry cash with you, use credit cards sparingly, and exchange currency at trustworthy banks or money changers. Always keep in mind that tipping is a personal choice and that the amount offered should be in line with the quality of the service received. By following these rules, visitors can have a good time in Bali and respect the people's hospitality and culture.

Chapter 12: Bali Travel Advice

Bali, an island in Indonesia, is well-known for its clean beaches, lush surroundings, rich cultural history, and exciting nightlife. It's the perfect location to unwind, relax, and become fully immersed in the community's culture. This page will summarize Bali's best experiences and attractions, offer more travel guidance, and discuss upcoming tourism-related changes and advancements in Bali.

Bali's Top Attractions and Experiences

Bali is renowned for its beautiful beaches, some of which include Kuta, Seminyak, Jimbaran, and Nusa Dua. These beaches provide beautiful views, silky sands, and waters that are crystal clear. Also, visitors can engage in aquatic sports including diving, snorkeling, and surfing.

Temples: There are numerous stunning temples in Bali, each with its distinctive architecture and background. Tanah Lot, Uluwatu, and Besakih are a few of the most well-known temples.

Rice terraces: Bali's rice terraces, a UNESCO World Heritage site, provide breathtaking vistas of the island's topography. Although the Tegalalang rice terrace is the most well-known, tourists can also visit the Jatiluwih and Pupuan rice terraces.

Volcanoes: Mount Batur and Mount Agung, Bali's two active volcanoes, provide breathtaking vistas and strenuous hikes. Tourists can go up Mount Batur to see the dawn or go on a guided tour of Mount Agung's crater.

Culture: Traditional dances, music, and festivals are all part of Bali's rich cultural legacy. Attending a dance performance or touring a nearby hamlet are two ways that tourists can learn about Balinese culture.

Food: Indian, Chinese, and Indonesian influences can all be found in Balinese food. Tourists can try regional cuisines including babi guling, sate, and nasi goreng (fried rice) (roast pig).

More Travel Tips and Advice for Bali

Transport: Traffic on Bali's highways can be hectic and congested. For island exploration, guests can either hire a driver or rent a scooter. Visitors should be warned that it's common for traffic laws to be broken and that the quality of the roads can vary.

Bali experiences two distinct seasons, the wet season (October to April), and the dry season (May to September). Visitors should be ready for unexpected downpours during the rainy season and extreme humidity all year round.

Bali is a mostly Hindu island, thus tourists should respect the regional traditions and customs. When visiting temples, dress modestly and stay away from public shows of affection.

Money: The Indonesian Rupiah (IDR) is the only form of payment accepted by the majority of establishments in Bali. Tourists should utilize ATMs in tourist locations and carry small banknotes and coins for transactions.

Safety: In general, Bali is a safe place to visit, but travelers should exercise caution by locking up their belongings and paying attention to their surroundings. Along with exercising caution when swimming in the ocean, visitors should steer clear of locations with strong currents.

Upcoming Changes and Innovations in Bali Tourism

The COVID-19 outbreak has had a substantial negative influence on Bali's tourism economy, and the island is currently experiencing a severe economic crisis. The community's government and tourism sector are making an effort to resurrect the sector and draw tourists to the island.

Sustainable tourism: Bali is dedicated to developing sustainable tourism and protecting its natural and cultural heritage. The regional government is putting eco-friendly procedures into place and attempting to lessen the damaging effects of tourism on the environment.

Tourism in Bali is adopting digitization to increase visitor numbers and improve visitor experiences. To make travel more convenient and accessible, many hotels and companies now provide online booking, virtual tours, and other digital services.

Infrastructure development: To better serve tourists, Bali's government aims to develop the island's infrastructure. This cntails constructing new airports, boosting public transportation, and enhancing roads.

Diversification of the tourism industry: Although Bali is best known for its beaches and cultural history, the local government is seeking to expand the island's tourism options. This includes encouraging eco-tourism, wellness travel, and adventure travel.

COVID-19 protocols: To safeguard the safety of visitors and residents, Bali has put strict COVID-19 protocols in place. This covers requirements for mask use, testing, and quarantine for newcomers, as well as social seclusion practices.

Final Thoughts and Bali Travel Advice

Bali is a stunning location offering attractions for all travelers, including pristine beaches, cultural landmarks, and delectable cuisine. But, travelers should be mindful of the difficulties associated with reaching an island destination, such as snarled traffic, cultural disparities, and unpredictable weather.

Take into account the following advice to get the most from your trip to Bali:

In advance: To save time and money, research the island's attractions and make an itinerary in advance.

Respect for the culture is expected of visitors because Bali has a vibrant and diverse culture.

Observe safety: Although Bali is a generally safe travel location, tourists should exercise caution.

Be environmentally aware: Bali is dedicated to encouraging sustainable tourism, and guests can play their part by adopting eco-friendly habits and minimizing their environmental impact.

Keep up with changes and developments: Because Bali's tourism sector is always changing, tourists should do the same.

In conclusion, Bali is a must-visit location for anyone looking for a distinctive and memorable travel experience. Bali offers something for everyone because of its breathtaking natural beauty, extensive cultural legacy, and dedication to sustainability.

Printed in Great Britain
by Amazon

29797417R0005€